MW01074680

<u>HOW TO QUIET YOUR MIND:</u>
Relax and Silence The Voice of Your Mind, Today!

MARC ALLEN

How To Quiet Your Mind: Relax and Silence The Voice of your Mind, Today!
Marc Allen

Copyright © 2011 by Empowerment Nation

Table of Contents

How to Quiet Your Mind: An Introduction

You might've heard the story before: a man goes walking through his neighborhood at night and comes across another man looking for something under a street-lamp.

"Can I help you find something?" The first man asks.
"I can't find my keys," the second man says.
"I see," says the second man. "I've dropped my keys out here before. I know what it's like. I'll help you find them."
"I didn't drop the keys out here," says the other man. "I dropped them on my porch. I'm just looking out here because the lighting is better."

As absurd as this story is, how many of us maintain exactly this sort of conversation with our *inner dialogue?* How many times did you, as a student, sit down to complete some important assignment, only to suddenly find something else (of far lesser importance) to attend to? How many times have you, in your adult life, been faced with some task or resolved to learn some new creative skill only to set it aside for some menial activity with no deadline or value? We've all been there. We've all been determined to do something important, only to be struck sidelong and taken off-task by some voice in our heads that encourages us to play this game or watch that show, or organize some part of our office that doesn't need it. After hours in front of the television spent flipping through substandard programming or perhaps even more time on the internet drifting from site to unnecessary site, suddenly it's time for bed and we've lost another day that we began with high expectations. Consider how many *meaningful things* you've tried to do that somehow became lost in a time-vortex of meaningless activity. It's not uncommon that after such a day we ask ourselves, *"Why did I do that? Why did I waste so much time?"*

The mechanisms that engage our inner dialogue go a long way toward enriching our experience as human beings, to be sure. They give us the ability to plan, anticipate, experiment, and come up with novel solutions to problems. Inner dialogue has been so successful throughout human existence, in fact, that it has devised an endless number of ways to avoid stressful situations in the modern era. The answer to "why" we procrastinate or otherwise fail to remain focused is actually quite simple: we're stressed. Some part of our mind suddenly finds itself in a situation of an unpleasant or undesirable nature and bails on us.

If the voices that distract us from work or otherwise important activities weren't bad enough, consider the converse situation. We've all been here too: it's the end of a long day, and you're simply trying to relax and reward yourself for time well-spent and jobs well-done, only your mind doesn't seem quite ready to shift into neutral. You perhaps find yourself stuck worrying about work when you should be enjoying time with your family or some activity that you take genuine pleasure from. This is the real tragedy of modern life. That same inner dialogue that guides us through challenging times, often with stunning grace and precision, can suddenly become trapped in a particular mode of exchange that no longer serves us once the challenges of the day have been met.

Most of us spend our lives struggling to deal with matters at hand in the present while half of our inner dialogue is pulling us into the past or pushing us into the future. Our mind is trying to take us anywhere but *right here and now*. We tend to worry about the future of a task or project before it is finished. We may even find reasons why such an undertaking will be obsolete upon its very completion. Again, how many times have each of us finished something difficult, only to discover it wasn't as necessary or important as we originally believed it would be? Doesn't that leave us crestfallen? But what is the point of badgering oneself about the fate of things we've completed in the past if there is nothing we can do to change it?

If it seems impossible to stop this inner conflict, that's with good cause. As stated before, the inner dialogue is part of the human condition. We're born with it and we use it so often that we're not aware of it—there's no way to permanently "dispose" of our inner dialogues. They are far too important to us. However, as luck would have it, you can *quiet it down*. You can work with it, even cooperate with it. You can even get *it* to cooperate with *you*, given enough practice. With patience and determination—

lots of determination, admittedly—you can learn this skill for yourself, and the benefits of doing so are seemingly endless. It's more appropriate to ask how quieting the mind *can't* benefit you, since it will leave you with a much smaller list.

This book is intended to introduce many of the benefits derived from quieting the mind. This is commonly done through meditation and other closely related practices. The reader will find it organized so that simpler techniques will be found before the more involved and time-consuming ones are covered. This should by no means discourage anyone from attempting and exploring all of these techniques, as the benefits derived from certain visualizations and mantras can far surpass simpler breathing-relaxation practices and quick stress release exercises. Suggestions and sources for additional information on the topics discussed herein may be found in some sections and readers are highly encouraged to take utmost advantage of their local libraries as well as the internet in order to cover many of these subjects in detail.

Quieting Your Inner Dialogue

It is advisable to start with simple changes here and there in order to develop a more helpful and communicative inner dialogue (i.e. one that isn't harping on you at seemingly every opportunity). Many times our minds are stressed because our bodies aren't being used in quite the way they were in past eras. In a similar vein, our minds are tackling problems and situations our ancestors probably never envisioned. Each of the exercises or habits explored below represents a very simple way to ease and quiet the mind on any given day, allowing one to focus when focus is necessary, and allowing a person to relax when he or she has earned it.

Of chief importance is for you to consider your own personal lifestyle and how you may be able to incorporate simple tasks throughout your schedule in order to relax the thoughts that ebb and flow throughout your mind. Some of these changes are seemingly obvious, but it is easy to overlook them on any given day. This is especially true if a busy routine gets in the way of your intent to quiet a noisy inner dialogue.

Below are several tips for developing new habits that foster a quieter, more cooperative and focused mind. These are some of the very simplest activities one can undertake in order to do so. Nearly all of them take advantage of the vaunted "mind/body connection" in order to relieve stress and increase focus. While any of these practices are relatively simple to engage in, none of them are necessarily easy to commit to. Any change in habits will be met with some degree of resistance or forgetfulness. It's important in this case not to succumb to frustration and abandon developing the new habit. Say, for example, that you discover the back-straightening exercise is very useful to you, but you realize at the end of the day that you haven't completed that activity. There's no need to become frustrated—and there's certainly no need to hoist yourself out of bed and force yourself through the routine if you'd rather go to sleep. Just make a quiet mental note to resume the practice upon waking up the next day in order to continue and *be sure to give thanks to your inner dialogue for the reminder*. Each of these activities is designed to quiet your mind, not upset it, so don't associate any of the techniques with *force* or you may come to resent them by that same association.

Straighten Your Back

Many of us have developed terrible posture practices over years, if not decades. Days spent in front of a computer screen hunched over in an office space can not only place stress on one's upper vertebrae, it can also lead to blockage of the air passages and decreased oxygen flow to the entire body. The more stress that builds in your body, the more your mind seeks some way to escape it or alleviate it. This is a big reason people can simply "blank out" in front of a computer screen after an hour or two of rigorous mental activity with virtually no physical movement. This represents to our inner dialogue that it is time for a break in such activities.

For an experiment, try resting your back on an exercise ball with your feet on the floor. Gently roll backwards (slowly to prevent yourself from losing balance) until your head is nearly upside-down. Once there, breathe in through your nose. If the increased intake in oxygen is obvious while you're effectively upside-down, it's a good bet that your back is hunched over through much of the day. Yoga—a practice we'll come back to many times here—is an excellent way to improve posture. A quick way to improve oxygen intake in the short-term is to sit directly on your hands and straighten your back as much as possible. Keep your neck as straight as it can be and breathe at your leisure. The difference is so noticeable you may feel the effects of this quick postural adjustment leak tension out of your upper and lower back for hours. Whatever the case, increased oxygen flow to the brain is a great starting point for a quieter inner dialogue.

Take a Break

This may seem obvious. Most of us are accustomed to a work environment that allows us several minutes to ourselves, every couple of hours. This allotment is generally mandated by law, but how we choose to spend this time can make the real difference. Time spent in a company break room amongst the chatter (and possible complaints) of other coworkers may better be spent reading a book and diverting your attention for those few precious minutes. Perhaps a breathing or relaxation exercise would better serve your purpose. People who enjoy sketching can perhaps cover a page or two in fifteen minutes if they find doing so brings them greater focus. Stress balls and "thera-putty" may seem trivial, but actually provide marvelous sensory experiences when taken advantage of, especially for people who tend to think kinesthetically. These activities are in fact so successful at quieting the mind that wide uses are made of them throughout autistic and other special needs populations. These activities help individuals who tend to become over-stimulated and distracted more easily than the general populace.

If, however, you genuinely look forward to your break so that you can converse with a favorite coworker or two—and if you truly feel refreshed and recharged after doing so—a break can still be made more advantageous by taking note of finer details. Perhaps the person you're conversing with looks or sounds different in some way. Questions such as "Is this person speaking faster or slower than they were yesterday?" or "Is so-and-so happier or more vital since the last time we spoke?" are great ways to ground a conversation in the moment. Making the effort to ask yourself such questions about people during a dialogue will also help prepare yourself to take stock of your own feelings and emotions.

However you spend your break, it is important to take ownership of it. Make sure it refreshes you and prepares you further for the rest of your day.

Keep a Schedule

Many of us begin our day with a fairly good notion of what we intend to accomplish in it, but it is always a good idea to keep track of what we actually have accomplished, what we still have yet to complete, and things that come up unexpectedly throughout the day. A simple schedule or list of things one intends to accomplish in a day can serve as a great centering tool for the mind. Consider checking items off as you complete them—sometimes even this small practice can significantly increase the satisfaction of a job well done.

You may also find that a large part of your stress stems from trying to fit a weeks' worth of accomplishments into a day or even an hour. If, for example, you write down twelve things you want to get done in a single day, and each of them will take roughly two hours, it's time for a quick reality check. It's a common experience to want to accomplish more than time will allow in one day, but it's good practice to keep your list reasonable, especially since distractions and changes are bound to occur. In this way, you are keeping yourself grounded in reality and communicating clear limits with your inner dialogue.

Don't become frustrated if everything you set out to do doesn't get completed in a single day. The purpose of this list is not to stress you out and aggravate your inner dialogue further. Instead, take a look at why one or several tasks remained left unfinished. Often, it amounts to unexpected changes or disruptions in your daily schedule. If that is the case, accept that such a change was beyond your control and consider ways to circumvent those changes from happening again. Sometimes this won't be possible, and that too is acceptable, since life happens whether we like it or not. If tasks weren't completed because of exhaustion or frustration generated by a frenetic inner dialogue, perhaps it's time to adopt a stronger method of meditation to put yourself in touch with the things going on inside of you that are inhibiting you from reaching your goals.

It's a good idea to jot down a very loose schedule for an entire day sometime in the morning or even the evening prior. Be sure to include one or two of the exercises listed here, since it may be easy to forget to quiet your mind throughout the day as you begin exploring these techniques, especially without a written reminder.

Find a Friend
Again, this strikes one as obvious. We're almost certain to turn to those we consider our friends when it comes time to vent or seek assistance in personal matters. But in matters of personal growth—and the ability to harness one's inner dialogue is at the core of just about any such undertaking—a closer examination of one's associates and cohorts can often reveal subtle facets of their personality. This will in turn allow you to reach conclusions about their individual suitability in aiding you with such a task. Does your friend listen, for example, until you are clearly finished saying what you intend to say? Or are

10

your talks with this person littered with interruptions? Does he or she respond with a story of something similar that he or she experienced? Is this friend's speech littered with platitudes such as "I know," or "things will all work out in the end" when you express worry, or does this person respond on some deeper level that resonates with you?

It's important not to look down on anyone who may engage in shallower types of conversation or behavior—because we've all been guilty of that from time to time—but it is also important to respect the limitations and abilities of others. In this vein, it is important to know and grow closer to those in your life that you respect for their communicative strengths. Learn from them. Do what you can to show them that you're really listening too. Again, this is more than just a common human courtesy; listening cooperatively with others is great practice for listening cooperatively with yourself.

A great place to find friends in your area if you are searching for a quieter mind will inevitably be a yoga or meditation class. People who attend these gatherings tend to be searching for inner quietude themselves, and have an uncanny knack for being open-minded and great listeners.

Exercise
This simple habit is often the most overlooked in one's day to day life. Sedentary persons are not exposed to the calming effect that a steady regiment of physical exercise can have on the mind. Walking

daily is naturally a good start to a life that includes a good workout and a quieter mind, but jogging and especially swimming are excellent ways to clear the brain of unnecessary worries. Of course, practitioners of yoga will swear by its mind-cleansing effects, which will be detailed in later sections. For now, it is important to be aware of the mind's close connection to the body. During and after any physical activity the body is releasing tension. The mind will unfailingly follow suit.

Fewer and fewer amongst us are manual laborers, and annual reports by federal health organizations can sound almost grim in their estimations of our collective amounts of physical activity. The obvious consequences—increased risk of heart disease, muscle attenuation, higher blood-pressure and cholesterol—can overshadow the mental deficits one can incur if physical activity is not pursued. As stated earlier, stress leads to muscle tension—particularly in the upper and lower back for many people. Physical activity forces the body to relax and release both the physical tension and mental stress.

Simple activities are a great start. Yoga and certain systems of the martial arts such as t'ai chi are excellent mind-centering tools, and can often be made use of during regular breaks in a schedule. For those with a predisposition for sports, consider things like tennis or badminton. Group sports can be a lot of fun, to be sure, but it's common enough to encounter boisterous or offensive team members on a basketball court or football field. These activities can unfortunately detract from the purposes of building a quieter mind, though if such activities are highly appealing, by all means participate in them and see what they can do for you.

Stretch

Stretching is just as important to the body as exercise. Ligaments tend to get impacted throughout the day, and they can entrap at least as much tension in the body as muscles do. As with exercise, stretching increases blood-flow throughout the body. Simple stretching guides are easily and readily available on the internet or at your local library. Take care to stretch gently and firmly—don't bounce or overextend any of your ligaments. This practice should certainly be done in tandem with exercising, as a failure to stretch can often result in injury and inhibit a person from participating in physical activities until fully recovered.

It's also important to stretch the entire body. Joggers may think only leg stretches are necessary, while those who have taken up rowing may simply focus on the arms. This is a common mistake that is caused by a misunderstanding of the bodies' muscle-use. Plenty of runners have incurred back or arm injuries during exercise, the reason being that even though those muscles aren't being used vigorously, they are still in constant motion during the workout. A stiff ligament can suddenly contract without warning during such activities. Exercise is also likely to create additional muscle-mass. This can cramp and inhibit tendons on its own, even if no obvious injury has occurred. Therefore, stretching is a must for anyone who engages in even the lightest of physical activities.

Scented Candles

Never underestimate the meditative powers of a small flickering flame. Certain scents (which scents exactly will vary from individual to individual) can serve as powerful mind-centering agents. Aromatherapy has been used as an alternative medicine for thousands of years, employing scented oils to alleviate stress, depression, anxiety, and a number of other emotional disorders. Varieties of these oils as well as scented candles can be found in health and beauty stores or natural food stores.

Simply light the candle, inhale deeply, and watch it flicker for a few minutes or so. If this is a routine that seems appealing, it's best to choose a single room in one's dwelling and make a regular habit of performing it there. As with many of the practices listed here, it is often beneficial to incorporate this technique into other forms of meditation. The breathing techniques listed below serve as excellent combinations with a flickering candle. It is often very helpful to pay particular attention to the scent of the candle; smells are processed in a very different region of the brain than sights or sounds. This region is located closer (and with easier access) to emotional centers. Thus, the right scent can serve as a very effective shortcut to a relaxed state of mind. Commonly used scents employed in aromatherapy include lavender, jasmine, chamomile, mint, thyme, and lemon. These particular aromas are noted for their abilities to release stress and anxiety, and to develop more positive moods. Do take care, however, to make sure the area you light the candle in is clear of flammable materials. The last thing anyone needs during a meditative experiment is an emergency situation in the home!

Candles work excellently after a hot-shower or during a hot bath if the luxury of time affords. Adding proper breathing (discussed below) to this combination does make for a very efficient mind-calming activity. This effect is so powerful, in fact, that researchers and meditators are still discovering various uses of the scent-based meditative practices. Scents are already known to be very powerful agents in the formation of memories and behavioral cues—consider, for example, entering a restaurant. If you're hungry enough, what does your stomach do the moment you walk inside and smell all of the food resting on the other diners' tables? To this end you can select a particular "trace scent" to use any time you wish to meditate. This will help your mind quiet itself more quickly.

Creative Activities
Painting, drawing, clay-sculpting, drafting, and other forms of craft have served meditative purposes since their inception. Everyone needs a creative outlet, and not everyone has one, or has made time available throughout the day to use it. These activities are especially meaningful for people

with a penchant for visual or kinesthetic activities. Taken even further, free-sketching and painting can clue the watchful observer (you, in this case) to recurring themes and modes of thinking in very subtle but powerful ways. This can be a very easy way to enhance the cooperative properties of one's inner dialogue in that it grants the unconscious mind another mode of communication. It has, in fact, been used in many forms of therapy for years.

Simply allow your hands to do the work. If a thought comes to mind, honor it, but there will be no need to force anything onto the page or into the clay. Just remember that you are communicating with yourself in everything that you create, then acknowledge and thank your inner dialogue for the assistance. A fully conscious understanding of what you've created will not be necessary—in fact, a more indirect and implicit knowledge of your creation will serve you better. Study your sketches or whatever you decide to do over time. Do they change over time or with your own moods and thoughts? Ask yourself questions about general impressions, what certain shapes or figures may mean if they keep recurring, especially if they seem vaguely familiar. A small amount of self-research based on your creations can reveal valuable personal insight.

Keep a Journal
For those of us not artistically inclined or who prefer word-based tasks, set a small amount of time aside in your day to record your inner dialogue. Though it may seem best or most convenient to do this activity in the evening, bear in mind this will also

be the time when you are most likely to be exhausted mentally. It is often difficult to develop new habits when the mind feels worn down, so the morning or afternoon—when there is a consistent lull in activities—may be a more successful time to develop this habit.

Keep your journal private, and don't judge whatever thoughts come to mind as you write them down. Habitual keepers of journals have been known to discover a wealth of personal knowledge that can serve them for years and beyond in their present lives. Some people will be stunned at the amount of situations and thoughts that once occupied their minds that seem trivial and insignificant years later. Others will find that they have been asking themselves the very same questions in different ways for years on end. These discoveries are only possible by keeping a written record, and will afford both the conscious mind and inner dialogues with a perspective on events in the present that is invaluable and otherwise unobtainable.

A specific type of journal—a dream journal—can offer the writer incredible mental insight. Such journals are often left next to the bed at night, and written in the moment one awakes. For those of us with difficulty remembering dreams, they can be a challenge to start, and people often become frustrated upon waking up and feeling the dream experience vanish from their thoughts. However, the steady and gentle determination to recall at least one dream a night can often lead to huge personal revelations.

Dreams are, in a sense, the continuation of one's inner dialogue while the conscious mind lies dormant. It is not uncommon—though it will manifest in different ways—for the active dreamer to learn to cope with a wide range of issues through the analysis of dreams.

Other Activities

It can't be stressed enough that you should never try to force yourself to achieve anything during this process, and that you should *have fun.* Don't be afraid to come up with new activities or hobbies if you find them appealing and calming. Perhaps building models is relaxing to you, or completing jigsaw puzzles or crossword puzzles. A newer popular activity is Sudoku. All of these activities and more have potentially powerful mind-quieting properties, and if you enjoy any of them, then by all means engage in them.

<u>Beginning Meditative Practices</u>

The previous list briefly introduced simple ways to change your daily schedule in order to better live in the moment. People can derive huge benefits from these small changes and activities, but why stop there if greater benefits are only slightly further ahead? Here, we begin to explore the first of what might be called genuinely meditative practices, and as with the previous list, different individuals may find some techniques more beneficial than others.

These techniques are by no means difficult to practice. They do, however, require the ability to set a schedule and stick to it. Early morning and afternoon meditations may be the easiest habits to develop, as fatigue may inhibit one's determination later in the evening. It is also very common for people to experience profoundly positive changes in emotional states and well-being upon first attempting them. This is all well and good—you deserve to enjoy your own life to your maximum capacity—but do bear in mind such techniques may suddenly turn stale or uninteresting from time to time. Before we explore the techniques, we should spend some time discussing how to interpret our results and feelings regarding their potential outcomes.

First, What Not to Do
Don't argue with yourself or try to force any experience out of your mind. Ever. Remember, if you meet with some kind of resistance along the way, that resistance is part of you and it is there for a reason.

We may not immediately understand or respect such limitations, but that is a reflection of what we have yet to learn about the process of meditation as opposed to what we are unable to accomplish.

If you try to meet any resisting aspect of yourself head on, you will lose. This is true of any task you set out to undertake. You might sit down in front of your computer with grim determination to finish a report your boss expects on Monday and growl at the protesting voice in your head. The odds are overwhelming that you will suddenly draw a blank the instant after you think you've successfully silenced your wayward mind. How many times do each of us tell ourselves to "deal with it" and wind up not being able to deal with it at all? Perhaps you even finish a bit of the work, but find your thought-engine grinding to a halt and falling apart shortly thereafter, leaving the task uncompleted. Whatever the case, by trying to *force* your way through a bout of procrastination, you will find yourself unsuccessful. In fact, that's why so many of us put things off and worry in the first place. Somehow, we've learned or been taught previously that the only way past a problem is *through it*. This may be true, but only after we have negotiated with whatever part of ourselves resistant to living in the now. No internal problem can effectively be dealt with simply by trying to force the mind to pull itself up by its own bootstraps—it just doesn't work that way.

It is of paramount importance to honor the reality that wherever that resisting voice seems to come from, it's really *coming from us*. Moreover, it's constantly working *for* us, doing the absolute best it can to help us avoid something even worse than procrastination or the inability to wind down at the end of a hectic day. It's constantly searching our future and seeking out ways to avoid failure. Think about it: it's hard to fail at something you don't actually do. The perfect time for our minds to search out and anticipate future possible failures is when nothing else is necessarily imperative (that is to say, when we're trying to relax). That voice is doing the very best it can to avoid displeasure, and sometimes it works so well that it prevents us from even trying. Now that we've covered how the process of learning meditation *should not work,* here are some ways and suggestions to glean more cooperation from the inner dialogue for the reader's consideration.

What to Do

There's one catch right off the bat: it's going to be different for every person. Some people will find the body-relaxation techniques listed below more helpful than others. Some will find that they receive huge benefits from the simple body tensing/relaxation technique listed directly below, while others may find similar advantages in adopting a breath-motion synching exercise or sensory-awareness technique. Each of us is different, and each of us will find different ways to inner quietude. The important thing, for those of us determined to silence the distractions we represent and create within ourselves, is to keep trying and, as stated above, not to fight ourselves.

There is a pivotal moment in many forms of Buddhism. It is not uncommon in any quest for self-improvement or self-enlightenment to come to a point of sheer frustration, or even despair, just before the inception of a major breakthrough. It is important as one begins this journey to remember that anything worth learning is not without its challenges and setbacks. If this weren't the case, we'd all have discovered this singular ability to quiet our minds on our own. And then, what would it really mean if we could all simply meander to the top of this spiritual hillside without facing challenges along the way?

Take a moment to picture what it is you want from life before you continue. Visualize it, write it down if you want to. Be specific. Maybe you want to master some form of creation—artistically, or musically. Maybe you want to write a novel. Do you want a better life for yourself or your family, regardless of what you have now? Do you want to grow professionally, or perhaps change professions entirely? Whatever it is that you want from life, the chances are your inner dialogue presently serves as an obstacle. Again—that is not an indictment of any part of your *self*. It is merely a statement of fact. Our minds were designed to help us cope with much simpler environments, and in their collective quest to do so, they have been overly successful in creating distractions and disruptions for all of us. Meditative techniques can clear away those distractions and disruptions and put us in touch with what's going on *inside*.

If you become frustrated or discouraged at any time, pay heed to that selfsame inner dialogue (it is *you*, after all) and feel free to experiment with and make changes to any of the techniques you find below. Don't sweat it, don't pass judgment on yourself, and don't try too hard. Quieting the mind and living in the moment is a constantly unfolding process of learning and adapting to suit one's own individual needs. It's your mind you'll be dealing with, so try to make it fun, engaging, and worthwhile for you. Stay playful with the experience, and you will be well served by it.

Basic Breathing

Breathing really is at the beginning of any meditation/relaxation technique you can engage in. Most of us have unconsciously adopted some of the worst breathing habits we possibly can. We spend the day expanding and contracting all that muscle and connective tissue (not to mention bone-mass) in our chests. If we become agitated or annoyed or otherwise excited, we suck air in quickly through our mouths and breathe it out like dragons.

Try this simple exercise: sit down on a comfortable chair for ten to twenty minutes. Breathe in slowly for three seconds. Once you have your air, hold it for another three seconds and then exhale for six seconds. Be sure that while you're doing this, your stomach is expanding as you breathe in and deflating as you breathe out. It's hard to believe we're actually *supposed* to breathe that way, isn't it?

Again, this is fundamental to any sort of meditation you wish to undertake. The better you get at it, the longer breaths you can take—some people are able to breathe in for five seconds, out for ten, and some are even better than that. Try to incorporate this type of breathing into any meditative activity you do—any activity you do at all, even. The mind/body connection is powerful, enough so that if your breathing isn't quite right, your inner voices will reflect that physical distress mentally.

Also be sure to monitor your breathing throughout the day. Does your chest feel loose or is it holding a lot of tension? If the latter is the case, redirect yourself to breathing calmly and properly, the difference will be immediately noticeable. Particularly long-term bad breathers may even be surprised to find that their lungs and ribs feel somewhat sore after they begin breathing properly. This is a lot like the mild aches one can develop after a work-out. The chest really should *not* be expanding and contracting with every breath we take—the abdomen should. It won't take long for your body to adjust, however, and rest-assured, you'll feel much better for having done so.

The Walk
This is perhaps the easiest meditative technique to engage in. While it may not serve many in the long-term, it is often an ideal starting-point for people with little time and inherent difficulties sitting still at the end of a long day. It involves just enough physical activity to remain engaging, and the mental

activities are enjoyed by many. Many schools of meditative thought also make use of walking and motion in more advanced techniques.

The technique goes as follows: find an area locally that you enjoy walking in. The fewer disruptions that are likely to occur along this walk, the better, but there are ways to cope with simple distractions below. Ideally this walk will take place from somewhere you can reach on foot. Once you are there, you do just that, *walk*. Take anywhere from fifteen to thirty minutes to do this.

There is a trick to it. If you're a fan of walking, you might already be aware of mentally tuning out while you do so. It's easy to let the mind wander wherever it wants while we're on a familiar path. With slight adjustments, an ordinary walk can become an effective meditative exercise. Instead of letting your thoughts wander without any direction, ask yourself, "What do I see?" Once you ask yourself this question, locate any object that stands out in front of you and ask yourself a detailed question, such as, "What color is it?" If you see a tree, ask yourself what kind of leaves it has, or what kind of bark, or how tall it is. If you see a fence, as yourself how long it appears to be, if it is well-kept or not, etc. If you're walking past houses, you can note simple details like the address numbers you are walking by, or whether the rooftops are wooden or slate. What are the exteriors of the houses made of? Are there power lines? Focus on what stands out for you. You'll find that this particular exercise becomes simple with a modicum of practice and diligence, and the more details you can register from a particular object, the more you are paying attention to your own perceptions and sensations—this skill is as important as appropriate breathing.

The point behind this exercise is to engage your inner dialogue with a simple task. If you can speak back and forth with yourself (not aloud, mind you!) in this fashion, you are re-building an important rapport with yourself. No doubt, you will find your thoughts wandering, either back or forth in time, as you begin this practice. If you catch your inner dialogue doing this, don't stress. Remember, those other little voices in your head are only trying to catch future or past errors and stop them from happening or analyze them in detail. When your thoughts wander, gently direct them back to the task at hand.

To this end, it can be very helpful to close your eyes briefly and pay attention to what you hear instead of what you see—just don't walk too long with your eyes closed! This may be especially helpful if you find yourself unable to pay attention to visual details for more than a few moments at a time. If you're not a visually-based thinker it may be more valuable for you to permanently pay attention to what you're hearing or feeling instead. If you're in a particularly playful or distracted mood during one of these walks, you can even pay attention to your thoughts. Try distancing yourself from the inner dialogue and commenting on it as a distinct entity from whatever words or images you experience along your walk. You might be surprised upon stepping back to see what your inner dialogue is really trying to say.

This is an exercise that works well for many just starting out or for those looking for a quick way to redirect their thoughts. It is best practiced after a long day at work during a lull when one isn't particularly distraught or excited. Louder inner dialogues are always accompanied by deeper emotional states, and stronger meditative techniques should be adopted accordingly. This exercise is designed to familiarize oneself with a very basic version of living in the moment. If you can familiarize yourself with a self-communicative task as simple as this, you've taken your first steps toward deeper meditation and a quieter mind.

Additionally, masters of meditative practices across the world will tell you that the purpose of any meditation is to remain in a state of mindfulness throughout the day, and not just when you are meditating. Walks of this nature prepare the beginner for that mindful state of awareness by placing their thoughts and inner dialogue in a state of living in the moment while being active. Ultimately, the goal of meditation is to remain in a meditative state your entire life, so walking and directing your thoughts in this manner are a great start to this habit.

The Muscle-Tensing/Relaxation Technique

Fewer relaxation techniques are as immediately effective as the tensing/relaxation technique. To engage in this technique, simply lie down on a comfortable floor or your bed (over the covers) and sequentially tense/relax each of your muscle groups. Start with your toes; curl them tight enough that you feel a moderate amount of pressure (stop immediately if you feel yourself any actual pain in order to avoid cramping). Hold your toes tight for fifteen to thirty seconds, whatever you have time for. Then, release the tension. Enjoy the sensation for several seconds, then proceed to flex your calves. Do the same thing to them (again, don't give yourself a cramp). Move up to your thigh muscles, then your stomach muscles, upper torso muscles, upper arms, forearms, then ball your hands into fists and relax them after the amount of time you've decided upon. Once there, clench your neck muscles by pressing your chin down gently (here more than anywhere else on your body should you be careful not to use too much pressure). After that, scrunch your face muscles into the tightest grimace you can muster and release.

The entire time you've been flexing and relaxing your muscles, you've also been engaging in a simple set of procedures very similar to the "walk" exercise listed above, with the added benefit that you've been using it to enjoy relaxing sensations kinesthetically. This exercise is an excellent release for those who hold lots of mental stress as physical tension, and can go a long way toward alleviating stiff backs and slow bodies at the end of a day. It's also a great way to start your morning: that tingling relaxation you feel is increased blood flow. You'll likely find yourself awake and alert, free from the need of your daily dose of coffee in the morning. This is also an excellent way to doze off to sleep at the end of a long day, as it will release all of the tension you have accumulated throughout it.

Breath/Motion Synchronization

Take the breathing technique listed above and incorporate some kind of repetitive motion into it—generally as simple as moving one hand back and forth—left as you breathe in, right as you breathe out. Pay attention to your heart rate, sensations in your moving hand and the rest of your body, all the while listening to the sound of your breathing. Keep whatever kind of motion you use small and synchronous with your breathing for ten to fifteen minutes.

This exercise has been known to have huge results in a single practice. Many will find it helpful to close their eyes and visualize their hand moving back and forth. This practice provides a powerful bridge in whatever communication gap you may be experiencing with your inner dialogue.

Other Mind-Quieting Techniques

Hypnosis: Despite our modernized society, hypnosis is often still regarded with suspicion and disdain. The reasons for this can easily be traced back to the founders of the practice, who often made farcical claims regarding the benefits of hypnosis.

Because of them, it is fair enough to say that certain uses of hypnosis are unethical and undesirable. With that out of the way, hypnosis actually bears a great deal in common with meditation. Those determined to quiet their minds would do well to check out the swarm of books available through their local bookstore or online in order to deal with the finer elements of auto-suggestion. One may even benefit from the use of a certified hypnotherapist. Those practicing hypnotherapy are very familiar with helping people find ways to relax themselves and assisting them in the quest for a quieter mind.

Hypnosis and meditation often work well-together hand in hand. Both are trance states, but subtle and not-so-subtle differences do exist between them. First and foremost, a person's heart rate tends to increase during a hypnotic induction, and while the benefits of both trances are similar, hypnosis is used to direct the mind toward solving a particular problem or alleviating a particular emotional state. The purpose of meditation is much broader, and while it is rare for people to spend hours on end in a hypnotic trance, often the very purpose of meditative practices is to hold such a mind state for very extended periods of time.

Hypnosis cannot force you to do something you deem immoral or undesirable, contrary to widely held opinions on the subject. It can help the entirety of your mind to synch up with itself and aid you in better achieving deeper meditative states, however. It is also highly useful in developing such habits, as it can often take a short-cut through all the mental roadblocks we've unknowingly erected throughout the years.

Binaural Beats: A little-known technique involving separate frequencies of sound in either ear has provided meditational benefits to individuals for decades. Though very little is known scientifically about how this procedure works, binaural beats have been shown to be able to relax the mind and improve focus, and different beats can have different effects on the mind. Though discovered in the mid-nineteenth century, the practice is still steeped in mystery, which means that many possible uses of binaural beats may still have yet to be discovered.

The general idea behind a "binaural beat" is that the hearing of two separate tones in either ear (through the use of headphones) produces the illusion of a beat. When used in meditation, this beat can be utilized to deepen the effects of relaxation. Most conveniently, these beats are readily available over the internet, often inside tracks with music designed to augment the meditation experience. A quick search online will reveal an overwhelming amount of information on the subject, including free binaural beats ready immediately for your own usage.

Remember, meditation is in large part self-experimentation with different sensory experiences. Binaural beats may end up being of great significance in your meditative journey. You may find that different frequencies of these beats yield vastly different effects. It is equally likely that some of the beats will help you when you wish to focus on some internal situation, and that others help you focus on the external world with greater clarity. The range and tempo of beats most effective for quieting the mind will vary from person to person—don't be afraid to explore and discover which ones are most effective for you. Just remember that these beats are effective only with headphones since the tone intended for one ear shouldn't be able to reach the other.

Going Deeper: Advanced Meditative Practices

Changing one's daily schedule to include small meditative tasks is one thing. Many who engage in the simple techniques listed previously will experience a drastic improvement in their quality of life. Their inner dialogue will come into focus and they will find themselves able to live in the moment as a result. With such simple efforts eventually yielding profound results, the next logical question to ask whether one can go even deeper. If the mind can be quieted to a manageable degree, allowing us more freedom of expression and direction, is it possible that we can completely silence the jumble of thoughts in our minds at any given moment?

The resounding answer is yes. In fact you've probably seen it happen before. Those of us who've spent much time on the beach have at least noticed all the people around them lying inert in the sand, if we haven't partaken of that extraordinary delight ourselves. If you've spent enough time around campfires, you'll notice people staring intently into the fire, and if you shake them gently, you may even startle them. Many of us can simply "tune-out" during long trips on the freeway. We'll appear asleep to the people around us, when in fact we're very aware of everything going on; we're simply detached. Alongside this feeling of being detached from surrounding events is the sensation of being *expanded*. The ebb-and-flow of the waves along the beach or the crackling hum of the fire or constant and rapid vibrations from a vehicle can often be *felt* from one in such a state, albeit indirectly.

The benefits of such experiences are clear to those who experience them. A few hours in a trance such and this clears the mind and relaxes the body to an incredible degree. The problem with experiences such as these is that they are situational. You can't always go to a beach or a campsite or get a friend to take you on a long drive. Besides, what we really want is not simply a situation that happens make our minds quiet. Instead, we want a method for doing so. For this we need a way of navigating through our inner dialogue and developing it to accommodate our needs as individuals. That's not to downplay the role of nature in meditation—being in a forest or meadow or beach can greatly enhance our experience. But we won't *always* be able to travel to such places. Again, quieting the mind can absolutely be done, and the benefits to learning the skill are seemingly endless to one who attains the knack—but you will need to work consistently for it. Progress from simpler techniques can have immediate results, but dedicated practitioners will find that the learning curve drops off for a while after the initial excitement of being able to quiet one's mind. Keep at it, keep trying new techniques, and above all, don't criticize yourself.

Practitioners of "serious" meditation often recognize it as an end unto itself, despite whatever benefits it may also grant a person. Those of us deeply engaged in the Western World of rapid commerce and exchange of information may find it difficult to comprehend the idea, but experts in the field of meditation (notably the Dalai Lama) are quick to point out that Americans are especially used to immediate gratification. We can't very well be expected to find the sort of inner quietude that seasoned veterans of the art have obtained after a lifetime spent meditating, if we only spend ten or twenty minutes a day in a light meditative trance. The real practice of meditation can take hours—even days or more.

Obviously, this represents a huge commitment that may not appeal to everyone, especially at first. But before the idea of practicing deep meditation is discarded, there are a number of important benefits to be considered.

Firstly, deeper meditation will achieve even more of what one was able to achieve with a light daily regimen. One can experience further reduced levels of stress (as the inner mind grows more closely linked to what we perceive as our "selves"). It can further improve our breathing habits, and goes a long way toward helping us stay healthy for longer periods of time as we grow older. Some research even suggests that meditation helps to eliminate the presence of free-radicals (known cancer-causing agents) in the body, reducing our chances of becoming ill and boosting our immune system.

Such practices also allow us to make better use of intellectual and creative capacities. The mind is a powerful instrument for change, and can grow to be more powerful with increased self-direction.

Besides all of these benefits to so-called *transcendental meditation*, the practice is very valuable in its own right. Each of our minds is a powerful place filled with near-infinite richness and mystery. Vacations to foreign countries often require long flights and an extended period of time set aside from work affairs, but deeper meditation techniques cost nothing. The sights, sounds and experiences you will undertake while in a true trance state are all the more valuable because they are *you*; they are transformative, and they will help you in every aspect of your outward life.

We measure the passage of time by discrete packets of events. We refer to happenings with words like "event," "occurrence," "action," "cause," and "effect." Our brain is constantly insisting that time is rigid and unfailing—alarm clocks, watches, and timers are produced by the millions and visible everywhere. It's no accident that the phrase "he/she wouldn't give me the time of day" conveys deep animosity to the person who has asked the question. One of the most significant changes one may experience during these deeper trance exercises is the growing sense that time is actually very dependent upon the observer. An hour or two spent in a deep trance can seemingly freeze time, and indeed it is critical during any of these exercises that one contemplates deeply on the meaning of time itself.

You'll come to find—with deeper and deeper levels of understanding as you explore—that what we experience as life is not, in fact, a series of distinct events, one happening directly after the other. The fabric of life—the universe itself—is constantly reforming and re-making itself. Change is the only thing that stays the same in our world, and anything that appears to exist here only exists inside that *constant flux of change*. This implicit understanding of universal nature will help you to confront even the most harrowing of challenges with a quiet mind.

Hence, not surprisingly, there's no set time limit to any of these techniques, as opposed to many of the moderate and simple ones listed before. The point with these exercises is to take as long as you can/need with them in order to explore your inner self. Don't set a timer to mark when you've finished. Conversely, don't force yourself to stay in a trance state if you feel it is time to resume other activities. And, don't be surprised if your sense of time is deeply affected by any of these exercises. A mere ten minutes will often feel like an hour or more, and that's a great way to start practicing with them. As you grow more accustomed and comfortable with each of these meditations, you'll find yourself able to spend more time and gather more knowledge and wisdom from them. Your first experiences may seem hazy or choppy—remember never to force anything. Go with it. If it seems like you aren't making progress, you may just be on the verge of an important breakthrough. The last thing you'd want to do in that situation is give up the practice. If you feel stuck, add or change another element. Perhaps a scented candle or binaural beat will assist in the further development of a trace state. Perhaps you discover a combination of two of the techniques listed below serves your needs better than either one individually. Go for it.

Meditative Positions

There are a huge number of meditative positions that have been developed throughout the centuries (and millennia). It is important, during your meditative practices, to become familiar and comfortable with one or two of them and make a habit of using them whenever you wish to go into a meditative state. Below are listed several of the most common positions for meditation. Note that they begin simply, with postures familiar to everyone. Be sure to try out the more advanced positions as well, since they are designed and developed for the purposes of increased awareness and breathing. These advanced postures will greater aid you in remaining awake and alert during your meditations, and many of them have a wide range of additional benefits to one's health and well-being.

These postures also have the additional advantage of signaling to the unconscious mind that an important dialogue is about to begin. They can also aid in gleaning further cooperation from it as you grow more and more accustomed to the position of your choice. In the same way that we unconsciously prepare ourselves for a drive when we sit down in front of a steering wheel, or ready ourselves for a meal by sitting at a certain seat at the table, these methods of sitting or posturing will ready our minds for the practice of meditation. You might also find it valuable to have several mirrors in your meditation space so that you can move easily in order to check that your posture is correct. It's very common to think that your back is as straight as possible when in fact it remains slightly crooked. Without seeing it for yourself, you can't be certain that you're in the pose completely. Combine these positions with the different techniques to discover what works best for you.

Lying Down

This is a good place to start when familiarizing oneself with meditative states. Simply lie down on your bed over the covers or on a safe place on the floor. You should work in a place that is free of other people and distractions. From here you can practice your breathing techniques and some of the more advanced activities below. This has the advantage of being easy to do, as virtually everyone lies down before going to sleep. As a result, it is quick to do and requires no concentration or energy.

However, there are some drawbacks to meditating in this fashion. It may be difficult to practice going into a trance by lying down after a long day at work. The mind is generally accustomed to falling asleep when we do this, so it is very likely that one will simply doze off in the middle of meditative thought. There's nothing inherently wrong with falling asleep while trying to engage in any form of meditation, but it might disrupt your sleep schedule later in the evening and will certainly make it more difficult for you to direct your conscious mind as you attempt to practice more difficult techniques. Additionally, it is common for small amounts of discomfort to become magnified during a meditative state, so if you plan to remain lying down while you meditate, you may need to spend some time locating the proper neck and head support so that you can remain comfortable. Visualization exercises are difficult to do with a severe crick in the neck or back spasm, so use caution. Notice also, that this technique is not suitable if you plan to incorporate movement into your meditation routine. Given that the more difficult forms of meditation can take hours to complete, lying down is almost certain to distract you from this goal. It will also be difficult to utilize external visuals unless you devise a method of hanging them from the ceiling above your eyes.

Still, this may be a good place to start for those who have decided to become serious about meditation, and may even be especially useful if you prefer meditative sessions before you go to sleep. If this turns out to be your preference, the convenience of drifting from a trance state directly into slumber will become obvious. The more difficult postures can be developed, perhaps by taking a yoga course or some other suitable class, and then implemented into your routine at your convenience.

Sitting

Here's another simple pose. Meditation can be done while fully seated in a relaxing chair, but for a more formal technique, try sitting on the edge of a chair instead, so that your thighs don't touch it. Keep your feet planted squarely on the ground in front of you so that your knees form right angles to the floor. Make sure your back is straight (*always* best for breathing) and that your head is slightly tucked-in to ensure the best maximal airflow. Relax your shoulders and rest your hands in your lap, palms face-down.

This allows the meditator to incorporate motions into his or her trance practices (as in the breath-motion synch exercise listed above). In a sitting position it is also easier to keep an eye on the flicker of a candle if you've decided for that to be an important part of your contemplative workout. Naturally, this position is far more preferable to lying down for serious trance-inductive work. It's far more difficult to fall asleep this way than lying down, and you'll be able to accomplish more as a result. This is also a good position to practice in if keeping your back straight and your chin tucked to your chest are skills you still need to learn for more formal stances.

Indian Style

This is another form of meditative posture that we are almost all familiar with. Sitting in this fashion requires space on the floor as a chair will make the position uncomfortable, especially if it is too small or has arms to it. Cross your shins and hold your legs together perpendicular to your back, which should be kept completely straight to prevent hunching over. Tuck each of your feet in. Each will go under the fold of the opposite knee, while the sides of your feet rest on the floor. Try to pull your lower legs towards your body as much as possible in order to straighten them out sideways from your torso. Your hands can then rest on your thighs or knees, or you can straighten both of your arms out so that your forearms are slanted toward the floor. Your elbows can rest on the side of your knees if you wish. Have your palms up and fingers curled inwards. Let your chin rest on the top of your chest for this position, as it will facilitate breathing. Be sure that when you breathe in, your abdomen is expanding and contracting as opposed to your chest muscles.

This is considered the first of the formal meditation poses. Please note that this position requires practice and patience. It will be very easy to allow your back to hunch over to begin with. It is also fairly easy to forget to pull your legs towards your body, and you may also notice one leg or perhaps even both begin to fall asleep in this pose. Given that blood-flow is an important part of successful meditation, it's a good idea to adopt an exercise regimen to try and increase your vascular system's ability to get oxygen where it needs to go. Your body will eventually become accustomed to sitting in this manner as long as you continue to adopt it during meditation practice, and in the long-term you will derive more benefits from it than lying down or sitting as listed above.

Sitting Crane/Kneeling

This is an unusual position for those of us unfamiliar with meditative practices, but it ensures full alertness. Extensive use of this position was made in feudal Japan and continues to be an important technique in the art of Zen. It is also difficult to master, and can be uncomfortable, at least while adjusting to it. In this position, the legs are not crossed. Instead, the knees rest on the floor in front of your body, side by side, and your lower legs are folded directly under them next to each other, so that your shins are resting along the floor. In essence, you are kneeling while keeping your back perpendicular to the floor. Your hands can either be turned upwards in your lap or resting on your knees. As always, your back is straight for improved posture and breathing, and of course, when you breathe, make sure you are using proper techniques. Let one toe rest on top of the other just behind your back.

This is another position that can be used in conjunction with any form of meditation that will require motion. As stated above, it can be difficult to learn to sit in this position for hours at a time, and it may be advisable to make use of a pillow or cushion to soften whatever surface you are sitting on. Again, be sure to check that your back is straight every couple of minutes or so—it's common when learning the *Sitting Crane* to let one's upper torso hunch over accidentally, especially after the first couple minutes of being situated in such a manner. Don't worry if it feels odd or uncomfortable to begin with. That means you're doing it right, and the awkward sensation will fade with more and more practice.

This is another position that lends itself to the use of visual aids and motion-based meditation, since the sitter will be unable to doze off as a result of the weight on his or her legs. It also takes up slightly less space, since the legs are situated directly under the body, so that this position can be adopted in more confined areas than Indian Style or the lotus poses discussed below. This can be a great technique to practice in a small meditative garden or another area where space is otherwise restricted.

Bow Position
This stance comes from yoga, and while it may be a difficult hold for the period of time required for deep meditation, it is a great way to begin relaxing the mind and body before a trance session. This is primarily the case because it reverses the stress we tend to place on our bodies by inverting positions we are most likely to take throughout the day (i.e. hunching forward). Begin by lying face-down on the floor and resting your hands with palms facing upwards. From there, bend your knees so that your legs come up into the air. Try to bring them as close to your hands as possible, because the next step is to reach backwards and grab them. Notice that this requires arching your back, so be sure to keep your spine and neck straight as you do so. Don't turn your head, and if you feel a sneeze or cough coming on, abandon the pose immediately. From here, pull your ankles towards the back of your head. This is a great

way to stretch out your chest and air passages. You'll find that it greatly increases comfort and flexibility as you continue to practice it.

Half-Lotus

This is a powerful meditative stance in its own right and a great preparation for the full-lotus technique listed below. Sit on the floor, very much like you would in the Indian style posture, only rest one of your feet on the inside of your thigh instead of placing it on the floor beneath you. Choose whichever foot you like to rest on the opposite thigh, whatever is more comfortable. The other foot can rest on the floor just underneath the opposing knee. Straighten your back as always, and extend your elbows so that your arms go out from your body straight. Keep your palms facing upwards while your fingers are curled towards each other. For the formal half-lotus position, have both your thumbs touch your index fingers.

This pose is very similar to sitting Indian style, but the added task of resting one's feet on the insides of the thigh can prove to require some additional flexibility. Again, it is easy to forget to keep your back straight, so while you are learning this pose be sure to check yourself from time to time in a mirror. Correct posture is vital to the success of any meditative undertaking. Poor blood flow or aching joints can bring one out of a trance or serve as an obstacle for deeper forms of meditation.

Lotus

This is exactly like the position listed above, save that it requires additional flexibility—so the *half-lotus* is a good way to build up to it. Instead of letting one foot rest on the floor, place both feet on the opposing thigh. This pose is perhaps the strongest of all meditative positions for fostering inner peace of mind and quieting your inner dialogue. It ensures full awareness is maintained throughout any trance technique, and will be slightly easier to adapt to in the long-term than the *sitting crane*. The lotus position is the most widely used technique throughout all schools of meditation and is by far the easiest pose to adopt for long periods of time. Certain schools of thought attribute to the lotus position an increased inner strength and health, as well as states of mind even deeper and profound than meditation.

Horse Stance

This is a common form of standing meditation, most widely made use of in T'ai chi. You'll want to stand with your feet shoulder's width apart and make sure your feet point straight ahead so that they are parallel to each other. From here, begin to bend your hips and knees as if you are going to sit down, but keep your back straight and head erect. Hold your arms out in front of you, slightly bowed outwards and make sure your elbows are facing the ground.

The *horse stance* is quite a workout, and a great way to stay healthy and keep the blood flowing while engaging in fairly rigorous exercise. For an even greater workout, spread your legs wider (or double the width of the imaginary horse) and hold this for as long as you can. It won't be long before your legs are shaking, especially the first couple of times that you try this. However, if you can remain focused on a meditation while engaged in this standing stance, you will certainly derive increased mental focus from it.

Empty Stance

Another common standing technique, this practice requires the meditator to stand with knees slightly bent, one leg out about six inches from the other. The feet should be angled slightly away from each other. Put about ninety percent of your weight on the foot closest to you and let the other one just barely touch the floor (this foot's heel should be off of the floor). Make sure your back is straight and your center of balance is curved so that your tailbone hangs inward. Arms should be up in front of you with your fingers spread apart gently, but make sure to leave your shoulders relaxed.

Common Deep-Trance Exercises

The 4-4-8 Procedure

This is a very common deep-trance technique. Choose the most comfortable meditating position you've discovered (from the ones listed above or elsewhere). Once situated, breathe deeply for four seconds. Hold your breath for another four seconds, and exhale for eight. This is similar to the basic breathing technique listed previously, but now we are going to add important visualization techniques to the mix.

Envision "healthy air." Give this vision some obvious quality as you are practicing your breathing. Perhaps it shimmers, is gold in color, or looks like bright blue liquid—don't pay too much attention to suggestions but use what works for you. As you inhale for the four seconds, visualize this air gathering around your mouth and nose as you inhale. Breathe the air in deeply and feel it cleansing and aiding your body. As you hold it there, envision this air filtering into your body through your lungs, and also envision the stress and tension inside of your body gathering in your lungs, getting ready to be expunged.

As you breathe out, don't be alarmed if the air you visualize is jet-black or green or some other pollutant-color. Don't forget, it's that ugly color because it needs to be ejected from your body in order to cleanse itself and become useful once more. Be sure you are feeling your abdomen expand and contract with every breath you take. Remember that you will feel better, more relaxed and refreshed, with every breath you take. Perhaps your blood begins to tingle with more energy as you do so. Perhaps you can envision yourself steadily glowing brighter as you take more and more of these cleansing breaths. Whatever the case, be sure to signal to yourself that you are growing healthier and more collected as you continue to breathe in this way. Visualize the bad air quickly dissipating as you exhale it, and immediately replacing itself with whatever visualization of healthy air you have selected.

There's no need to adhere strictly to the 4-4-8 inhalation/exhalation routine in this breathing exercise, especially after you are comfortable with it. Breathing in and holding it for a set amount of time is a good way to build a steady habit of taking in the right amount of breath at first, but you'll rapidly adjust to whatever pace you need for this technique to be most effective for you. It is also a great exercise to maintain good physical health in general, as the visualizations within are greatly encouraging to the body's immune and vascular systems. Imagining yourself growing healthier can go a long way to actually feeling and being healthier. It's a fantastic trance induction to incur after a rigorous workout or long day at work, when extra care and attention may be of greatest benefit to the lungs.

It is the added visualization that makes this otherwise simple breathing technique into a powerful meditative tool. The body responds well to such internal representations, and as you practice, you will find your unconscious mind grows increasingly responsive to these changes. Common aches and pains found in the body will readily begin to heal themselves and begin to disappear entirely.

I Am

Begin this exercise with muscle relaxation—the tensing/relaxation exercise listed previously is suitable here. Once you have done this, assume your favorite meditative position and continue to relax while controlling your breathing and taking account of your surroundings.

Close your eyes and take note of what you see inside of your eyelids. Pay careful attention to how the images are always changing. The same images will never occur to you again so long as you live, so take great care to pay as much attention to them as you can. Contemplate on the nature of continual change, and think on the things that you see throughout the day. Do they ever stay the same?

Next, concentrate on what you hear. Even in a silent room we can still hear sounds from our own bodies. Pay close attention to the fact that what you are hearing is constantly changing, just as whatever you see is constantly reforming and recreating itself.

After sights and sounds, pay attention to what you smell and taste. Similarly note that these senses are in a constant state of flux as well.

After smell and taste, continue with what you feel—on your skin and inside your body. This too is impermanent, and in a constant state of change.

Finish with taking stock of your thoughts and your inner dialogue. Here, more than any other aspect of the mind save perhaps for sight, is that constant state of change obvious and tangible.

Be sure to contemplate on each of the senses and your thoughts sufficiently to understand the nature of their changes. Do this each time you perform this exercise. Once you've done this to the satisfaction of you and your inner dialogue, it's time for an important question.

Ask yourself, after taking note of what you sense and feel and think, if you have had this experience as the same person who experienced things yesterday. Then, ask yourself, if you are still the same person who just took note of all those sensations and thoughts. The obvious answer will be yes, but that's not the answer you're looking for. And, sorry, you're not looking for a simple "no," either.

Continue to think about how everything around you has changed in just a short time, and yet you feel unique and unchanged throughout. Think about your concept of "same" as opposed to "different" or "changing." Here's the final question to ponder: How is it in this world of constant change that you as an individual experience one moment to the next, as if you were the same person from one moment to the next?

The answers found by practitioners of this technique will be more beneficial from experiencing the technique itself than they would be from merely reading them. In fact, if it were even possible to see the answers on this page, they would do you little or no good. Your inner dialogue will bestow these answers with playful subtleties that words on a page will not be able to emulate. This exercise is a fantastic way to synch up communication lines with your inner dialogue. Note the similarities to the walk exercise listed at the beginning of this book. They are almost the same thing, except with *I Am*, you are commenting on the nature of your own perceptions, rather than merely perceiving. This exercise, then, takes the experience of sensation to the next level, as you more deeply contemplate the nature of a constantly shifting reality. This deeper level increases the benefits of the meditative practice accordingly. With steady practice you can take this inner learning outside the meditative state and begin to experience your day to day world on a more profound level.

Will Power Concentration

A very common use of deeper forms of meditation involves the increase of what we call "will power." Recall, a major benefit of being able to quiet the mind is to allow increasingly larger portions of your mind to cooperate with your more overt and conscious intentions.

To start, use the *schedule* discussed above. It is a good idea to write the next day's objectives and desires down, in order to meditate on them before you go to sleep. This will allow you time to think further on them as you drift off to sleep—but remember, you are not worrying about them. Maybe you are contemplating why these things are important to you; perhaps you are visualizing yourself completing the tasks with ease, or imagining an inevitable interruption and seeing yourself deal with it gracefully and competently. Whatever you do, remember the words of Confucius, who said "If a problem can be solved, why worry? If a problem cannot be solved, then worrying will do no good."

Here's a good way to complete this meditation. Once you've finished your list, get into your favorite meditative position, relax, and visualize the list in your mind. Take the first task, say it out loud to yourself, and ask yourself if the task makes you nervous or uneasy for any reason whatsoever. If not, it will be simple enough for you to imagine— with enough detail as possible—completing the task with ease. It's important to remember here that even though you are trying to remember as much detail as you can, there's no need to spend an inordinate amount of time visualizing each individual task. Simply imagine going through whatever stages of the task you deem appropriate and wait for your inner voice's approval. This serves as a signal to the person meditating that the unconscious mind understands what has been asked of it and will do its best to comply. The "best" offered by our unconscious minds is always better than we could otherwise hope for.

Once you have visualized this task, move on to the second. Again, pay close attention to the details. You will come to notice that "you" are partially creating these scenes, while what you perceive as something else is filling in the setting or adding details. Make an effort to notice your surroundings, especially if something that doesn't seem critical to the task at hand stands out. For example, say that one of your goals is to find an appropriate gift for an anniversary or birthday. To do this, you will likely visualize yourself inside a store, searching for something the recipient will enjoy. You might know the object you're searching for to begin with, or you may ask your inner dialogue for assistance in the matter. If the latter is the case, pay attention to people your inner dialogue might send your way to assist you, or objects or colors that continue to "pop" out at you during your visualization. These small details represent significant attempts at communication from your subtler mind, which often tries to relay complex information in images such as these.

You won't always be able to consciously determine what the information represents explicitly, but that's not your primary concern. Your goal in paying attention to these details is self-exploration and understanding, which comes with time and practice such as this. After you've become sufficiently familiar with certain cues from your unconscious (don't get discouraged, but it will most likely take years), you will be able to take these deeper images with you as you return to conscious activity and utilize them with great effectiveness.

This technique also lends itself to the completion of long-term goals that can take days, months, or even years to complete. As you become more familiar with your own meditative style, you will be able to contemplate more expansive goals such as learning a musical instrument, owning your own successful business, or writing that screenplay or novel from the idea you've had for years.

The Meditation Garden

This exercise is a significant change in anyone's life, even for those who already possess a green thumb. It takes advantage of our inherent inclination to relax and slow our minds down when in the presence of nature. An appropriate meditation garden represents years, sometimes decades of silent determination and self-exploration. The garden itself will never be complete. It will continue to require constant maintenance, and you may find yourself constantly changing and rearranging patterns, plants, and decorations within the area you've designated. Let this serve you as a constant reminder that the world never stays the same.

First, imagine (with the aid of other forms of meditation) what you are going to want in your garden. What kind of flowers do you want, for example? Do you prefer plants that will bear edible fruit during a given season? What kinds of scents do you want present in your garden? Do you see trees, and if so, what kind are they? Take time to consider all these aspects of your garden, along with what kinds of decorations and arrangements you'll want once you get started. Maybe you have space for a small decorative shed outside that you can place the garden inside, or you decide you'd like a small pond to overlook during meditative practices. Go online to see what others have done with spaces similar to yours and compare what you imagine with what they've been able to accomplish. It might be a good time to head to the library to check out books on gardening, taking care to select texts with the strongest visual aids.

Take into account the size of garden you will reasonably be able to maintain. For many of us, this could be as simple as a square plot in our backyards no larger than a few yards. Those of us with acres at our disposal will be able to take even more considerations into account, such as how quiet or far away from roads the area is, or what the view from beyond the garden will look like.

Once you've come up with your plan and gathered everything you will need to assemble your area—it's a good idea to keep things simple at first—you are ready to begin. Create the garden in whatever increments are conducive to your schedule, and be sure to spend time meditating and contemplating inside the garden before it blooms. As with *I Am*, this will serve as a powerful reminder that the world is in a constant state of change.

As time passes inside your garden, you will find it a perfect place to practice a wide range of meditations. The "other" voices present during our inner dialogues are like "us" in many respects—most importantly, they benefit from habit and routine. The more inner communication that occurs in this specific area, the more cooperation one can expect from our inner selves within it. In time, the inner dialogue will eventually silence itself inside this garden, given a simple request. This is a powerful signal of self-trust and self-confidence, since it signifies that your unconscious mind has grown to understand that this silence is critical to your well-being as a whole.

Zen Gardens, or Japanese rock gardens, are a terrific start for those with little time or space to create a thriving landscape. These simple gardens can consist of nothing more than a few square feet, sand, rocks, and a rake. The sand is meant to represent water, and the raking of the sand is meant to rearrange symbolic waves inside the sand itself. Self-starting rock garden kits are available all across the United States, and are a terrific way to explore the inner and outer nature of change with minimal distraction.

The Descartes Meditations
Surprisingly enough, a somewhat common form of deep meditation stems from a prominent mathematician and philosopher from the West (recall

that meditation is a very potent tool for increasing one's intellectual and creative abilities). René Descartes, dubbed the "Father of Modern Philosophy," introduced a treatise that lends itself as a helpful guide and tool for self-meditation. With a few simple modifications, the material within is really the stuff of all meditative practice. *Meditations on First Philosophy* is very useful in its own right, and it may even be advisable to locate a translated copy for reference. Such a guide will not be difficult to find, and different translations might even provide different insights as one will always vary in content slightly from another.

This meditation will require you to record a great deal of your own thinking, either with a digital recorder or pen-and-paper journal. Revisit this work and add to it frequently, familiarizing yourself with everything you've written or otherwise recorded will facilitate the work you will do in meditation. As with the *garden*, this exercise represents years of self-exploration and personal work to achieve greater understanding.

To begin this meditation, start cataloguing the beliefs you've held about your *self* and the world in general since early childhood. There will be many of them. Are there things you think you are incapable of accomplishing? Determine the things you think are immutable in the world. This is a good time to consider undesirable patterns of your own behavior and the behaviors of those around you. Think of what you know about these behaviors, and, more importantly, what you don't know. It's almost a certain guarantee that you will be unable, at least at first, to determine why you or others engage in these behaviors.

Consider everything you can during this first phase and take as much time as you need and more. Once you've thoroughly taken account of everything you feel appropriate, make a conscious determination to suspend your beliefs about the world around you. It won't be uncommon to meet some resistance from your unconscious mind as your inner dialogue attempts to squabble with you. Remember, the job of your inner voices is to keep your view of the world consistent with your experience. For example, if you consider yourself to be a shy person in social settings, understand that your unconscious mind goes a long way to bolster this belief in order to protect you from becoming embarrassed or ashamed in these situations. In this light, the unconscious part of your inner dialogue is discouraging you from participating with friends or new acquaintances in order to protect you from things it may perceive to be harmful or even devastating. That's a laudable goal, to be sure, but for now simply remind yourself that this exercise is essentially a game, and no harm can possibly come from imagining a world where things or people might suddenly behave in a different way. For the example above, this would mean imagining a world where you perceive yourself as affable and greatly enjoy the company of others. Just ask your other voice to play along and give it and you the satisfaction of a fun night out with friends or being the center of a conversation, however imaginary. It will be useful in the long run, to be certain.

Second, after you've taken all of these beliefs into account, consider the most important aspect of your experience. This is what Descartes called the "I" of experience. What is it about you that makes you who you are? Don't expect or try to formulate a simple answer. Again, when dealing with your inner dialogue, the answers you glean from them may seem hazy or murky and very subtle at first. There's no problem with this. Part of the reason we are exploring the nature of constant change and mystery in the universe is to be able to derive meaning from the shifting and unclear answers we might receive after we ask such questions. These seemingly confusing images or feelings are in actuality the essence of life and livelihood in this world of ours. We must grow comfortable with them rather than attempt to force them to behave in whatever way we wish. As astounding and as capable as our minds are, our beliefs and thoughts about absolutely everything are riddled with perceptual and philosophical errors. It follows logically that the inner search for your "*I*" will not result in immediate enlightenment. Remember you're in it for the long-haul and be prepared to play with the idea for years, possibly. The point of this phase is for you to suspend your beliefs about what makes you, "*you.*"

Third, you will want to organize your thoughts, beliefs and emotions into separate categories. You will find in your perceptions about yourself and the world around you that they possess the qualities of *volitions* (actions), *affections* (habits), or *judgments* (beliefs). Volitions represent physical events that appear to transpire, from the traveling of light from the sun to the earth to our acts of greeting people with a wave or smile. Affections represent patterns of both actions and judgments in the universe and in ourselves; they are what we perceive as recurring events and emotions. Judgments represent our internal evaluations of perception. They are the emotional and rational reactions we have to whatever transpires around us.

These are important categories to recognize and to foster in our daily lives, primarily because we tend to blend *volitions* so heavily with *judgments* that we can easily confuse one for the other. In the example above, a person who constantly confuses the *volition* of having difficulty talking in a social situation with the *judgment* that they are poor performers in such situations is selling himself or herself short by failing to separate the two categories. It is much more worthwhile to perceive such a situation as an opportunity to invoke the nature of change and attempt to thrive in communication with others by considering the *judgment* that there is something to be learned by participating in such a situation. The conclusion that Descartes was led to, and the lesson we are trying to understand during this involved form of meditation, is that it is very possible we are deceived with respect to what we think are basic components of the universe. For Descartes, it was the possibility that mathematics was flawed. For you, the revelations may be of a more personal nature.

For the fourth phase of this work, again consider the nature of your own existence and the things you *know* to be true. For example, how is it that you know a book or rock will fall if you drop it? If this is a false assumption, how is it that you are able to predict accurately each time you perform this action, that the object will drop? Another contemplative question during this meditation goes as follows: upon meeting up with a close friend or relative, you always *know* who this person is. Again, ask yourself, has there or could there ever be a situation in which this is false? Here we are contemplating the core of uncertainty and trying to understand that despite the nature of constant change as the essence of our world, somehow we come to depend on apparently stable elements within it. Think of some negative impression that you have of yourself or the world at large that you would like to see change. Where does it come from? If humans are so good at being able to depend on stable principles and objects in a constantly changing environment, what leads us to misconception and misunderstanding?

The fifth phase consists of considering whether the attributes given to objects and ideas would still exist without your perception of them. A square has four sides, by definition. Would that be the case if you didn't exist? Take these questions wherever you like, especially inwards. If, for example, you didn't perceive yourself to act in a certain way, would you still in fact behave in that fashion? This is an important puzzle for each of us to solve individually, as it is certainly true that our moods, outlooks, and perception of events can be influenced by the internal beliefs we hold about ourselves. If those beliefs didn't exist, what kinds of changes would we then be capable of achieving?

The sixth and final phase leads the meditator to examine the distinction between the mind, body, and external objects. For example, consider where your *mind* ends and your *body* begins. It may seem simpler, at least at first, to distinguish inanimate objects from your body, but think carefully on the subject. For example, nearly everything in our bodies has been discarded and replaced within the last eight weeks. If there is such a distinction between us and the food that we eat or the air that we breathe, how is it that this inanimate matter is constantly replacing microscopic pieces of our bodies that no longer serve a function?

Descartes reached a number of profound conclusions based on these questions. Yours may be different from the seventeenth century philosopher's, of course, but this manner of thinking is composed of precisely the deep and life-enriching questions that will help you in your quest for enlightenment.

Five Element Meditation

For this technique, first assume your favorite meditative position and utilize proper breathing. Calm your thoughts, and when you are ready, consider the four elements, or states of matter. This is another form of "deep thought" meditation, and you will find some of the same themes here that were found in the above meditation based on Descartes' philosophical essays. Go through each of the elements, one at a time, and consider their role in your existence and in the existence of the world around you.

Start with earth. This element represents hardness. Rock, metal, dirt, and sand are all forms of the earth element. Contemplate the element of earth, then think about its role in your body. Bones, nails, and other hard tissues are all composed from this element. Consider that all of these things from the element of earth, that now compose pieces of *you*, were once something else entirely and will someday be something else entirely again.

Next, move to water. Blood comes from this element, as does the fluid in every one of our cells. Consider how all of the liquids within us are constantly diminishing and replenishing, as old blood gets recycled and fluids leave our bodies. As with earth, the water element within us is in a constant state of flux. It did not begin as a part of us, and it will not end as a part of us.

After earth and water, consider the element of air. Air is constantly entering and leaving our lungs. As it enters, we take in oxygen that we cannot live without. As is exits, toxins to the body leave with it. We would not be able to survive without this bodily function. Think of air, constantly entering and leaving your body. As with earth and water, it does not stay with us for long.

Now, think of fire, or energy. Each of our brain cells depends on small electric discharges to communicate with surrounding cells. Muscle cells function the same way. Each of our cells constantly utilizes food (earth), air, and water to create this energy in order that we may live. This energy is constantly flowing into us and out of us. It is the most basic function of life itself. Without this motion of energy, nothing would be possible. Consider, too, how this energy comes to be inside of you and comes to leave you.

Now consider your consciousness, that constant ebb and flow of thoughts in your mind. Though we experience ourselves as a unified whole, consider whether your thoughts are the same as they were yesterday, or even from moment to moment. The entirety of what it means to be human rests on the idea that we call *consciousness*, but in fact this is really just as impermanent and changing as everything else around us.

Notice that none of these things are ever really created or destroyed—they are merely changed. Again, change is the only permanence within the universe, and nothing is ever the same from moment to moment.

Big Mind Meditation

This technique, on the surface, appears to be the opposite of quieting the mind, but as you go into a deeper trance, you will discover nothing could be further from the truth. As it turns out, letting your inner voices run rampant for a short time can assist you further in communicating with them.

Get into your best stance, and relax. Let the flow of your thoughts go wherever you want for a short while. Then, when you are ready, start up a conversation with your "Big Mind." Envision this "Big Mind" as the thing responsible for controlling each of the voices and thoughts running through your head. This is the essence of you and everything inside both your conscious and unconscious thoughts.

Remember, this is essentially your *boss*. While speaking to it, remain respectful and don't try to force anything on it. By definition, the Big Mind is more powerful than whatever voice you have chosen to use in order to communicate with it, and you share every interest mutually with it besides. Ask it questions about who it is, and want it wants. Generally these things will be in your awareness without having to wait for the answers, but ask anyway. Sometimes the Big Mind will have very different plans for you than you have for yourself. If that is the case, listen, discuss the matter, and come to some kind of cooperative conclusion.

Once you feel comfortable conversing in this fashion with your Big Mind, you can ask (again, gently) to take its place for a while. This is tantamount for requesting permission to be in complete control of yourself. From here, you can converse more easily and fluidly with different aspects of you and your thoughts.

Now it's time to get creative and generative. What do you want to change about yourself? Find a voice in your thoughts that appears to be impeding that change, or could possibly help you accomplish such a change with a few modifications. Speak with it rationally—don't try to bully or cajole anything from the voice. Come to an understanding of this voice's purpose in your mind, and try to negotiate another way it could serve that same purpose without inhibiting yourself as a whole or your goals.

Spend as much time as you want in the place of the Big Mind. Talk to whatever voices you deem appropriate while in meditation. You may even find it wise to mediate between voices in situations where a dilemma or some other choice has come up and you are unclear on which path you wish to take. Simply listen to both sides of the argument, represented by different and opposing voices. From there, make an effort to ensure the voices have both been heard, by yourself and by each other. Make sure neither voice harbors any negative feelings towards the other, and come to a conclusion that satisfies both, or at least offends neither.

You'll find that working through problems in this way is surprisingly easy to do once you've learned to meditate deeply enough. We spend far too much time hemming and hawing over decisions throughout our day-to-day lives without attempting to negotiate through them peacefully. In this fashion, you can go a long way toward ensuring that your mind remains sound throughout whatever transition you've decided upon. You'll find far less in the way of regret or remorse for paths not taken.

Mantra Meditation
This form of meditation is almost diametrically opposed to Descartes' formulation of thoughts and philosophies, but it is by no means less important or powerful to an individual who decides to undertake the study.

A mantra is a simple word or phrase repeated to one's self while in a meditative position. The object of this practice is to concentrate on this singular word or phrase and block out all other awareness. This is one of the oldest known forms of meditation, predating Buddhism by centuries at least.

There is no limit to what you can select as your mantra, so long as it resonates deeply enough with you and serves your purposes well. It should be a short phrase, able to be memorized instantly, and it should possess a cadence or rhythm that lends itself strongly to proper breathing. There are nearly endless common mantras developed by masters of the art, but consider developing your own, perhaps after some practice with them. Technically speaking, a mantra doesn't even have to be a real word. So long as it sounds *right*, go with it.

Astral Projection

The practice of astral projection is thousands of years old, and while it requires a great deal of mental concentration and dedication, solid practitioners of meditation consider it one of the most sophisticated and worthwhile techniques available to mankind.

To begin this exercise, sit in a comfortable position (a good chair will work, but a stance from yoga will work better). Close your eyes and make sure that you are breathing regularly and naturally, as described in detail above. Relax for a bit, and pay attention to the sounds around you and inside of you. Note the feel of your clothes against your skin, and the current of air against your face and arms.

Next, try to visualize yourself sitting there meditating, as though you were standing as an observer about ten feet away. Note the expression on your face, and watch your diaphragm rise and fall as you breathe in and out. Give your visualization as much detail as you can, such as what state your hair is in, what your clothes look like, even what small involuntary twitches to the body (there may be a few) look like as they happen.

Now comes the tricky part, where we invoke the ancient concept of the astral body. This is theoretically a body contained within our own, composed of matter subtle enough not to reflect ordinary light and also capable of passing through objects. Visualize this body—your astral body—rising up and floating above your meditating self. Though many texts and reports exist denoting the coloration or appearance of such bodies, you might find it more beneficial to "allow" your astral body to take on whatever appearance it deems necessary. Simply allow whatever your astral body looks like to rise up, and float just below the ceiling.

Take a moment to study your astral body as you would study anyone that you've just met. Next, move your visualization toward it slowly until you are inside of it. Once inside your astral body, glance down and see what you and the rest of the room looks like from the ceiling.

From there, take flight. Remember, this body you've put yourself in has the ability to fly through solid matter, so go ahead and float right through the ceiling. From here you can get creative, and (it can't be said enough), do not pass judgment on the experience. As you float out of your neighborhood to wherever you wish to go, if you're discouraged by the fact that you don't know details such as whether this house or that actually has a pool or large tree in its backyard, remember that it doesn't matter for the purposes of this exercise. You're playing a complex game with yourself that rests on visualization and attention to your own inner details. It's fine if your astral body sees things differently than your regular body would—it's composed of different material and bound to interpret its surroundings a little differently anyhow, right?

Beginners often find themselves instantly pulled to a place they think of, even if they don't recognize it. That's fantastic—the astral body can travel instantaneously, after all. Still, if the experience seems jarring, simply take a moment to register your surroundings. Don't force anything to happen, don't keep anything from happening. Just take whatever is happening into account and explore patiently.

There is no limit to what you can explore with this exercise. At first, images may seem "weak" or flimsy in some way. This is simply because we are not accustomed to taking such great care to visualize our internal experiences. As you practice this and other forms of meditation, you will be increasingly able to fill that absent space in your mind with profound thoughts and internal experiences of this nature. Colors and sounds will grow to become more vibrant the more you engage in this visualization exercise. You will find yourself constantly surprised and moved by the images you can evoke with this method. Eventually, you may wish to allow yourself to be pulled to other regions of the galaxy or universe. Why wouldn't you? It's not as though we have a better way to get there!

In fact, this method can grow to be so powerful that a slight caution should be noted here, before we continue. Encounters with other entities while in astral form can seem threatening and confusing, but they are not dangerous. It is impossible to die or even become physically harmed from the result of travelling in the ,astral body. Moreover, you can end the experience any time you wish. Simply stand your real body up and continue your day, if needed—though the traditional end to this exercise is to imagine yourself being pulled back into your actual body and making a conscious effort to incorporate what the astral body has learned during the experience. Astral travel is so very different from our waking state of mind that it is easy to lose material from the experience during the transition, much as it is in dreams.

Schools of Meditation

While the information found in this book will be useful in your search for inner quiet, it is always advisable to continue learning and incorporating more knowledge into your meditative practices. To this end, there are a whole swarm of different meditative philosophies for the individual to explore. It is highly advisable to take a look around and see what's available in your area. Most schools offer free trial classes, and the added benefits of being in a group with like-minded individuals will doubtless enrich your life and lead to new insights regarding the nature of inner peace and living in the moment. On top of this, a savvy course instructor can assist you in the finer points of trace-posture, induction, and self-guided contemplation more that any amount of writing on the subject can compare.

This is by no means a comprehensive list of everything available to those interested in furthering their meditative practices. The art of meditation is so ingrained within the fabric of human existence, every culture and society possesses its own particular variant. Each of these variations is rich and full of its own idioms and practices. Typically, these schools are infused with religious practices and customs of their own—but don't let this discourage you from trying something out just because it might be "different" from the religion or customs you grew up with. These new teachings can only serve to augment your own religious and philosophical understandings of the world around you, and will only be a force for the positive in your life.

A note on each of these practices: all forms of meditation possess nuances and terminology particular to their origins within the cultures that commonly practice them. The amount of language and subtle variation of word-meanings in each school of thought can be baffling to all but the most knowledgeable scholars. In an attempt to avoid such confusion, complex terminology has not been made use of. This list is meant to briefly introduce some of the more common forms of meditation, using words that a native English-speaker would be familiar with. For example, a word meaning "empty," in many of these languages can also take on the meaning of "clear," "free," and "unobstructed." No such word exists in the English language, so a quick translation of this and any of the words native to these practices would only do the reader a major disservice.

Yoga
The word "yoga" is nearly synonymous with meditation. The practice is thousands of years old, and its focus is on blending physical stamina and flexibility with a clear mind and spiritual well-being. Courses on yoga can be found throughout the United States with ease. Many of these offer their first course for free. Many are inexpensive, and for those with more financial flexibility, instructors are available for one-on-one sessions. Yoga is a definite must for those wishing to enhance their meditative experience, and will offer health benefits ranging

from boosted immune systems to healthier blood-pressure and beyond.

Qigong

This meditative practice stems partly from the teachings of Confucius, though its roots recede far into ancient Chinese and Indian histories. Qigong focuses on quieting the mind through mental focus combined with various physical stances and postures. It shares much in common with yoga and other forms of meditation, at least on the surface. Many of the stances in Qigong involve standing postures, and the meditative technique will often require the practitioner to focus or visualize some place or object while engaging in some kind of repetitive motion.

This is another excellent physical practice, aside from being a good way to meditate and sharpen one's mental focus. Qigong is also an important part of many martial arts practices, and some research suggests that it is particularly useful when recovering from a sport injury or other physical trauma. A great deal of variation of the main principles of Qigong exists, primarily since it was practiced all throughout various regions of China.

Qigong has been much more commonly practiced in the United States and other Western nations since the 1990s. It may be more difficult to find a class that explicitly practices the art, but t'ai chi courses make extensive use of the meditative techniques found in Qigong, and they are almost always readily available in any region.

Zen

This art flourished in ancient Japan for centuries, though it began in China centuries before that. As with most meditative arts, its historical origins are blended with legends and unverifiable stories that were passed on from generation to generation orally.

Primary practices in Zen range from sitting and focusing mentally on various issues, to puzzling over complicated verbal stories and answering questions with no obvious answers. If you've ever been asked what the sound of one hand clapping is, or whether a tree falling in the forest with no one around still makes noise, you're familiar with two of these types of riddles. The point of these questions is not to discover a direct, obvious answer—in fact, if you do, it's an indication that you have a lot of meditative work to do yet.

Zen has a wildly impressive tradition of stories and legends associated with it. The relationships between Zen-masters and their disciples are often the source of these legends. Many of the stories are humorous and engaging, filled with insight and incredibly deep character sketches. Each of the masters deals with the questions from his disciples in various ways, and the disciples are almost always asking their masters the wrong questions, or seeking the wrong answers. One disciple is thrown over a bridge by his master after trying to *become one* with the coldness of the water at a distance. Another Zen master has his tools hidden from him as his disciples grow worried that he is too old to work. When he stops eating as a result, they give the tools back to him. He resumes eating and working. To his disciples he says simply, "No work, no food."

The path toward enlightenment in Zen emphasizes a constant exchange between confusion and clarity—the acceptance and understanding of this dynamic force is the essence of Zen meditation.

Christian Mediation

It is a mistake to assume that simply because the Christian religion is of more Western origins that it does not possess a formal school of meditative thought. Indeed, the tradition of Christian meditation is just as rich and vital as any other, and should not be overlooked in one's quest for enlightenment, especially for those amongst us already belonging to the Christian faith and seeking to deepen those ties and better ourselves as a result.

Christian meditation most commonly involves prayer while focusing on important passages of the Bible and contemplating their meaning. This is meant to bring the meditator closer to himself while also joining in communion with the divine source of creation. This communion invokes the concept of the Holy Spirit—the essence of the divine present within each of us.

Many practitioners of Eastern meditation argue that the use of the Bible is a significant departure from formal meditative practices, which attempt to clear one's mind of all inner thoughts. However, this criticism can hardly be valid when so many methodologies of meditation already utilize clearing one's mind by filling it with philosophical or religious knowledge. Conversely, practitioners and experts on Christian meditation often make serious attempts to distinguish their forms and techniques from those in Eastern religions and philosophies.

While it is certainly true that a person who practices Christian meditation will do so in a vastly different fashion than a practitioner of Zen or yoga, it is also equally true that Eastern schools of thought have vastly differentiated their own practices as well. The dichotomy between "East" and "West" is far more illusory than most are prepared to accept.

Other Forms of Meditation
There are countless less-known forms of meditation throughout the world, from the shamanic drum rituals found throughout the Americas to the dreamtime dance rituals practiced in aboriginal Australia. Tibetan sorcerers devote their lives to profound meditative practices and develop incredible mental and physical discipline as a result. For these shamans and priests, the very purpose of life is perfection of their meditative arts. Herein lies an important message to those of us just beginning to learn the secrets of trance induction. Some people have become so adept quieting their inner dialogue that they have come to understand that the purpose of meditation is meditation itself.

This way of life is vastly different from typical modernity. The Western world tends to focus on prospect of a better future, with quicker rewards and improvements always being preferred over long-term benefits provided by things like meditation. Our society seems to be increasingly poor at things like time management and organization as we become more skilled at losing ourselves in unproductive distractions like video games or celebrity gossip. One thing all forms of meditation will accomplish is to provide a set of implicit skills and mindsets to safeguard against being lost in the endless sea of distraction we perceive around us, and within us!

Despite subtle individual differences, each form of meditation shares a great deal in common the practice as a whole. To those who insist on believing that Western thought is vastly different from conceptions of Eastern philosophy, a quick examination of Marcus Aurelius' *Meditations* will serve as evidence to the contrary. Many of the ideas in this work are parallel (if not identical) to much of the philosophy of Zen Buddhism. *Meditations* is not the only book that shares a great deal in common with Eastern philosophy. Each of the major schools of classical thought draws from the same philosophical wells as yoga, for example. Important writings from prominent physicists such as Neils Bohr and David Bohm explore the inner nature of the universe and have gone so far as to advance theories suggesting that our perception of the universe around plays a much larger role in its constant reformation than we may realize. If that sounds familiar, it's because common forms of meditation approach this conundrum from a different perspective. The forms of meditation may be different, but the function is always the same. The essence of focusing on inner thoughts and quieting the mind is there in all forms of mediation regardless of where they come from.

A Final Note on Quieting the Mind

Using the examples, information and techniques in this book, anyone can begin to practice quieting their mind. As you begin your first simple meditative practices, remember that you are learning what it means to have a quiet mind. Take care to remind yourself gently that such learning will sometimes come easily, but it will also take time to master. The small changes you make to your way of life and schedule will slowly re-teach your mind how to experience the world around you. It is very likely, upon making meditation a habit, that you will suddenly "realize" one day that you have become a much stronger, more relaxed person than you were months or years before. Be prepared for many such revelations, as the meditating mind is one constantly improving and enriching itself.

Much of the time you once lost by dwelling on the past or fretting about the future will become time spent in the *now*, getting things done with an inner dialogue that is on your side. You will find yourself engaging in tasks and activities with ease that once would have caused you great inner turmoil and stress—and isn't *that* a reason to begin meditative practices on its own? Imagine something you want to do now but feel you can't for whatever reason. Meditation really can, with time, give you the strength to do such things easily and well.

One final consideration on quieting the mind: our society is experiencing profound changes on an incredible scale. The internet came into use barely over two decades ago, and has been growing faster and more effective and spreading more information ever since. Cellular phones arrived on the scene shortly thereafter. The two revolutions recently merged in the form of smart-phones, which has again changed the nature of our society. Search engines like Yahoo and Google provide us with instant access to any kind of knowledge we might hope to seek, while GPS devices prevent millions from becoming lost every hour.

These are arguably positive changes. You might find yourself at a loss to remember how you used to perform tasks such as meeting someone in public or finding a restaurant in a different city without a cell-phone. That's all well and good, but the same devices we use to make our lives better can also be used to burn inordinate amounts of time playing pointless games or looking up useless information. Meditation is always time well-spent, and steady practice will lead us away from such petty engagements and ensure that our time on this earth— admittedly shorter than most of us would like—is well-spent.

Visit

http://www.EmpowermentNation.com

to view other fantastic books, sign up
for book alerts, giveaways, and updates!

20501183R00049

Made in the USA
Lexington, KY
07 February 2013